50 ZAPPIEST BIBLE STORIES

50 ZAPPIEST BIBLE STORIES

Andy Robb

CWR

Intro

Welcome to 50 Zappiest Bible Stories!

Now, you're probably wondering how on earth a Bible story can be 'zappy', aren't you? Thought so. Let me explain…

The Holy Spirit is God, and the Bible tells us that there were many times when God gave certain people some of His power to help them do stuff for Him. Because the Holy Spirit is so powerful, those people probably felt like they were being zapped by God – so that's why this book is called what it is. Just so you know, 'zapped' isn't a word you'll find in the Bible, but you get the idea!

That said, not every experience of the Holy Spirit is 'zappy' (in fact, some are quite ordinary!), and you'll get to hear about some of the other amazing ways that the Holy Spirit showed up in the Bible as you read on.

Before we start, there's one important thing you need to know about God, and it's this. Although there's just one God, the Bible tells us that God is in fact three persons:

Father God, Jesus and the Holy Spirit.

To prevent your brain from exploding trying to work this out, it's probably best that you simply take the Bible's word for it. Lots of grown-ups, pastors, teachers and very clever people are still trying to understand what we call the Trinity (God being three persons) – perhaps it's just too much for our human brains! So let's agree that God is God, and the Holy Spirit is a part of who He is.

If you've never so much as taken a sneaky peek between the covers of a Bible (and even if you have), it's sometimes really head-scratchingly tricky to know where exactly to begin. For starters, the Bible isn't one big book – it's lots of smaller books (66, actually) that are all crammed together like a mini-library. The books have all got fancy names, such as Genesis (which is right at the very beginning), Job (pronounced JOBE), Psalms (pronounced SARMS), Mark (which you'll be relieved to know is actually pronounced MARK), Habakkuk (which should get you a pretty good score in a game of Scrabble) and Revelation (which is right at the very end).

Just to make it even more complicated, some of the books have got more than one section (like a sort of Part One and Part Two), and each Bible book doesn't just have chapters like normal books do – it has verses as well (like you get in some poems).

So, if you wanted to have a read of verse 7 of chapter 20 of the second book of Kings (because there are two of them), you may find it written like this...

2 Kings 20:7

…which, to me, looks more like a maths equation than anything to do with the Bible – but that's the way it is!

If you're itching to know what the Bible reference I just used is all about – and also to find out how some perfectly good figs were (in my opinion) wasted – then you're going to need to get your hands on a copy of the Bible to check it out. In fact, you'll need a Bible to get the most out of this book so beg, borrow or buy yourself one as soon as you can.

As it's not always easy to decide which bit of the Bible to read first and in what order you should read it, we've gone and done all the hard work for you. Aren't we kind?! In this book are 50 hand-picked Bible stories, which are retold in a zappy style and with a colourful cartoon to stop you getting bored. At the end of each story, you'll get the chance to find out what happens next (we don't tell you, you've got to do that for yourself!), and that's when you get to use your Bible. Using the info that we give you about where to find the story in the Bible, you'll need to look it up and then see how the story finishes.

We've jumbled up the Old and New Testament stories, so remember the Old Testament all happened before Jesus came.

That's about it.

Off you go and happy reading!

1
HOLY HOVERER

If you know anything about the Bible, the chances are you'll know that the very first book is called Genesis. The name of this Bible book is a whopping big clue as to what it's about, because Genesis actually means 'the beginning'. And who do you think is there, right at the start of everything? Yep, you guessed it! The Holy Spirit, the star of this book.

The Bible doesn't always call Him the Holy Spirit. Sometimes He goes by the name of 'the Spirit' or 'the Spirit of God', which is how He's referred to in the Bible bit I'm going to tell you about now.

Once upon a time, there was absolutely nothing. No planet Earth, and no universe surrounding it. There was just God in heaven. Then God did something amazing! Out of nothing, He created the whole, huge universe.

But there was still work to be done. The world was really not much to look at – just a lifeless planet covered in water. Not for long, though! The Bible says that the Spirit of God was hovering over the earth. Why was that? Our special planet was going to be home to people like you and me – but first, God needed to make it *feel* like home. For the next six days, God created everything in nature you could possibly think of, from flowers and trees to birds and bees. You name it, God made it!

Not only is God's creation amazing, but so is the way that God made it. God simply commanded things to come to life and they did. As the words left His mouth, it was the Holy Spirit who made things happen. That's why the Bible says that He'd been hovering over the earth. The Holy Spirit had been waiting for God to speak, and when He did, the Holy Spirit sprang into action!

BEZ IS THE BEST

Did you know that God likes camping?! Well, He does! In Bible book Exodus you'll find loads of stuff about a very special tent that God instructed the Israelites to build, just for Him.

Here's a bit of the background to the story. The Israelites were on their way to a land that God had given them to live in. The journey should have taken them a couple of weeks, but it ended up taking them 40 years (but that's another story).

Because the Israelites were always on the move, they lived in tents – which were easy to set up and easy to take down. The Israelites were God's special nation, so wherever they went, He went.

One day, God told their leader, Moses, that He wanted to live among them. Wow! What an awesome privilege. But hang on a minute… Surely God wasn't planning to live in one of the Israelite tents, was He?! No, He most certainly wasn't. God had something a little grander in mind.

The tent that God told Moses to build would be the most magnificent tent imaginable. It was called the Tabernacle, and measured 45 feet (that's nearly 14 metres) by 15 feet (roughly four and a half metres).

Not only did God give Moses detailed instructions about what the tent and the furnishings should look like, but He handpicked the guy who was to head up the whole thing.

His name was Bezalel, and God had given this guy wisdom and skill to work with gold, silver, bronze, stone and wood. Everything in the Tabernacle had to be tip-top quality, and Bezalel was the man to make sure that happened.

If you're wondering what this story has to do with the Holy Spirit, I'll tell you. Although Bezalel was a good craftsman already, God filled him with His Holy Spirit to make him an absolutely brilliant one so that the Tabernacle would be a tent fit for God.

Want to find out the name of the man God chose to be Bezalel's right-hand man? Head to Exodus 31:6.

MAN PLAN

od must have had so much fun making the universe –
imagining all the wonderful things He was going to create,
and then bringing them to life for real! Bible book Genesis is
where you can find the account of how God created everything.

To save you having to look it up for yourself, I can tell
you that God made everything by simply commanding it to
happen. For instance, God commanded the sea to be full of
living creatures and sure enough, that's what happened. Bible
book Genesis is where you'll also get to discover how long it
all took (six days from start to finish, if you're interested). Not
only was the Holy Spirit actively involved in all of this, but
there was one more really important job left for Him to do.

God was about to make the world's very first man (Adam),
but He wasn't going to make him in the same way that He'd
made everything else. If you're a dab hand at pottery (or
know someone who is) you'll know that it takes a lot of skill
to produce a beautiful pot or plate from a lump of wet clay.
As weird as it might sound, God was also planning to make
Adam from nothing more than a handful of dirt (I'm guessing
that the soil was moist to help shape the man, but the Bible
doesn't actually say so).

As wonderful as a dirt-man made by God might be, he wouldn't be very good at looking after the world that God had kindly made for him. He'd be little more than a lifeless statue, which frankly wouldn't much use to anyone. Fortunately for us, God knew that.

Time for the Holy Spirit to do His stuff.

The Bible says that God breathed His life (the Holy Spirit) into the man, and Adam came to life!

You can find out how God made a wife for Adam in Genesis 2:18–22.

4
FABULOUSLY FAST PHIL

I'm not trying to scare you or make you nervous, but did you know that God sees everything? That's what the Bible tells us. It also says that God knows what we're going to say even before we open our mouths, and that He knows how many hairs are on our heads! God doesn't want to know those sort of things about us because He's nosey, but because He genuinely cares about every single detail of our lives. And that's why this next zappy Bible story is particularly fascinating!

The church in Jerusalem was being given a hard time by people who didn't like what they believed, and many of them had left in a hurry. One of them was Philip. He'd ended up in a place called Samaria, where he spent his time telling people about Jesus and doing miracles in God's power. And now, God had another job for him.

An angel showed up and instructed Philip to head off on a certain road out in the desert. Philip did what any sensible person would do if an angel from God gave them an order – he obeyed. Philip hot-footed it to the place he'd been directed to and waited to find out what he was to do next.

Soon enough, a smart chariot appeared, and in it sat the chief treasurer (fancy!) of Queen Candace of Ethiopia (that's in Africa if you didn't know). He was heading home after a trip to Jerusalem, and was reading from Bible book Isaiah.

Now this is the point at which the Holy Spirit got involved and told Philip to chase after the man. Philip must have been pretty fit because he caught up with the chariot and got invited in to explain what the Bible passage meant.

Because of Philip's super-fast running and crystal-clear explaining, the Ethiopian official came to believe that Jesus is the Son of God. And all because one man did what the Holy Spirit told him! How's that for encouragement?! Let's be listening out for what the Holy Spirit tells us to do!

To find out about the unusual ending to this story, go to Acts 8:36–40.

5
HEADING HOME

Nobody likes having to say goodbye, and it can't have been easy for Jesus to have to tell His disciples – His very best friends and students – that in a short while He would be returning to heaven. It had taken most of the disciples quite a while to realise that Jesus was more than just an amazing man who taught with authority and healed people of sicknesses that nobody else could cure.

The penny had finally dropped that Jesus was also the Son of God, who'd been sent to earth to get us back to being friends with Him. But having spent over three years with these guys, Jesus now dropped the bombshell that He would be leaving.

No way! What would they do without Him?!

Fear not! Jesus had already thought of that. Here's the thing. Although thousands and thousands of people got to see Jesus close up or at a distance, it was always going to be impossible for everyone on planet Earth to meet Him. And that's not forgetting those of us who were born years later. There was zero chance *we'd* ever get to see Him face-to-face.

And so, as Jesus prepared to head home to heaven, the Holy Spirit was waiting in the wings, ready for a signal from Father God. Jesus informed His disciples that, once He'd gone back

to heaven, Father God was going to send the Holy Spirit so that not only would they not be left alone, but neither would anyone else. That included everyone alive at the time, and everyone who would ever live after that.

That's not all! There was a difference in the way people would be able to relate to God because the Holy Spirit was coming. When the Holy Spirit came, He would come to live in everyone who was a follower of Jesus. People would actually have God inside them. Wow!

Head to John 14:26 to find out a couple of things the Holy Spirit would do when He came.

GIDEON GULPS

When you read through the Bible, you'll notice that God has a way of choosing people to do stuff for Him who often don't think they're up to it.

Gideon was one such man. He lived in Israel, but God had removed His protection from the nation because the Israelites had turned their back on God. For seven years the Midianites had been making their life a misery. Finally, the Israelites came to their senses and cried out to God for help. They realised that they did need God after all.

God is extremely patient, and He answered their prayers by raising up a leader who would defeat the meanie Midianites. His name was Gideon – but there was just one *teensy* little problem – Gideon was a bit of a scaredy-cat. When an angel showed up to announce to Gideon that he'd been handpicked by God to lead the Israelites to victory, Gideon was petrified. Gulp! Surely God had got the wrong man.

'But how can I rescue Israel? My clan is the weakest one in Manasseh, and everyone else in my family is more important than I am…' was how Gideon put it.

The angel assured Gideon that God was going to give him

Holy Spirit power, and that he wasn't going to have to do this in his own strength.

God was as good as His word. As Gideon prepared for battle the Holy Spirit zapped him (came upon him) and he blew his trumpet to rally the Israelite troops ready for war. But later that night, doubt once again set in, and Gideon asked God for more proof that he really was going to rescue Israel. Sure enough, God obliged and Gideon was finally convinced.

As the Israelites went off to battle, God had a surprise for Gideon. So that his army of over 30,000 didn't get the idea that they'd defeated the Midianites in their own strength, God whittled the army down to just 300 men. Just 300!

And with the Holy Spirit to help them, Gideon and his tiny army were victorious.

If you want to discover the bizarre way they won the battle, you can find the story in Judges 7:16–22.

7
FRUITFUL FOLLOWERS

Have you ever watched a fruit tree blossom and then show the first signs of fruit forming? It's pretty cool – but fruit trees are *supposed* to bear fruit, aren't they?! That's their job!

But what if I said that you and I are also meant to bear fruit? You'd probably think I was a bit odd, wouldn't you? Well, for the record I'm not odd and, strange as it might sound, the Bible backs me up about what I said.

In Bible book Galatians, Paul (who wrote it) was trying to explain how when a person has the Holy Spirit living inside them, their behaviour will change for the better. He hit on the idea of saying that it was like God growing fruit on the inside of you.

Because the Holy Spirit is God, He's loving, joyful, peace-loving, patient, gentle, good and faithful.

When someone becomes a follower of Jesus, the Holy Spirit not only comes to live inside them, but that person gets the chance to allow the Holy Spirit's life to flow through them as well. And that means that *they* can also be loving, joyful, peace-loving, patient, gentle, good and faithful. Paul calls each of these things the fruit of the Holy Spirit.

How can you get Holy Spirit fruit to grow in your life? If we skip back a few verses in this Bible bit from Galatians, Paul gives us some handy hints – which basically boil down to making some good choices.

Rather than doing and saying bad stuff that can hurt others, we can choose to allow the Holy Spirit's life inside us to influence what we say and what we do. The more we do this, the more we become like the Holy Spirit and end up treating people like He would. How cool is that?!

Jesus also said something about how we should treat other people. Find out what it was in Mark 12:31.

8

JC'S JD

When you're all grown up, the time will come when you'll need to apply for a job. Most jobs have what's called a job description (or 'JD'), which tells you what you'll have to do if you get the job.

But did you know that Jesus Christ had a JD? Yep, He did!

If you know anything about Jesus, there's every chance you'll know that He was God's one and only Son who'd come to earth to patch things up between us and God. Although God had created the world and put us in charge, we'd made a bit of a mess of things and had, for the most part, cut God out of the picture. Without God in our lives, things had gone from bad to worse. Instead of being a happy place, the world became filled with things that made people's lives miserable – such as sickness, anger, hatred, jealousy and all kinds of wickedness. This is why God sent Jesus. Jesus' mission was not only to get us back to being friends with God, but to get rid of all that bad stuff which living without God has allowed in.

So, right at the start of His ministry, Jesus made a beeline for a synagogue (a Jewish church) in Nazareth and spelled out why He'd come, and what His JD was:

'The Spirit of the Lord is upon me, because he has chosen me to bring good news to the poor. He has sent me to proclaim liberty to the captives and recovery of sight to the blind; to set free the oppressed and announce that the time has come when the Lord will save his people.' (You can find that bit in the Bible in Luke 4:18–19.)

But did you notice the reason Jesus was going to be able to accomplish His mission? It was because the Holy Spirit (the Lord's Spirit) would be helping Him.

9
WISE UP!

Because the Holy Spirit is God, when He comes upon a person or into a person, they receive all that God is. Because God is love, they will feel loved. Because God is powerful, they will feel protected. Because God is wise, they will be wiser. That's exactly what happened to King Solomon. He'd taken over the job of ruling Israel from his dad, King David.

Solomon's dad and God were the best of friends, so following in his footsteps wasn't going to be easy – and Solomon knew it. By all accounts, Solomon was quite young when he became king and he wasted no time in asking for God's help to rule Israel. To be precise, King Solomon asked God for wisdom. And how does God download wisdom? By the Holy Spirit, who the Bible also calls the 'Spirit of Wisdom'.

If you're wondering how Israel's new king used his Holy Spirit wisdom, I'll tell you. One day, two women came to him with a bit of a dilemma. They lived in the same house and had both given birth to babies within three days of each other. Sadly, one of the babies had died, and its mother, desperate for a child, swapped the babies, hoping she wouldn't be found out. But she was. The other mum knew she'd been tricked and that the other mother had *her* baby. She wanted her baby back

– so they'd come to King Solomon to sort everything out.

While the women argued back and forth in front of the king, Solomon thought about what to do. The Holy Spirit zapped him with His wisdom – and he knew what to do! King Solomon came up with a rather clever idea that would settle this difficult dispute once and for all.

WAIT FOR IT!

Before Jesus returned to heaven, He had some final instructions for His disciples – but they weren't what you might have imagined. Having spent three years training His trusty band of followers (the disciples) to teach people about God and to heal the sick, you'd have thought that Jesus would want them to get on with things as quickly as possible once He'd left the earth.

Nope! His instructions were to wait in Jerusalem.

Wait? What for? With Jesus gone, shouldn't they get busy carrying on where He left off? Well, yes and no.

Yes, because of course Jesus wanted them to continue being His witnesses… but no, because they'd not yet received the power of the Holy Spirit to enable them to do this. This was the reason Jesus had commanded them to wait. God was shortly going to pour His Holy Spirit on them so that they'd have the same power to do the things that Jesus did.

And with that, Jesus returned to heaven.

A few days later, while the disciples were praying together and waiting for what Jesus had promised, a sound like a rushing wind filled the room that they were in. Before they'd had the chance to catch their breath, what looked like tongues of fire came to rest on their heads. The wind and the fire were just signs that Jesus was as good as His word – and that they were being filled with the Holy Spirit!

There was so much commotion that people outside wondered what on earth was happening! The disciples were so overwhelmed by the wonderful experience of being filled with the Holy Spirit that some people actually thought they were drunk!

11
SUPERNATURAL SPEECH

How would you like to speak another language without having to spend time learning it? Sounds cool, doesn't it? Well, that's exactly what happened when Jesus' disciples were filled with the Holy Spirit!

When they opened their mouths to speak, it wasn't their native language that came out – but the languages of the people from other places who were visiting their city of Jerusalem!

Understandably these visitors were more than a little surprised by what they heard, but it was God's way of letting them know that He loved them – He spoke to each of them in their own language.

The Bible calls this 'speaking in tongues', and it isn't freaky in the least when you understand what it's all about. When we are filled with the Holy Spirit, we get the chance to allow God to express Himself through us in what we think, what we do and what we say. Sometimes it will be in a language people understand (like in this story) and sometimes not.

Sometimes, if we find it difficult to love people, we need the Holy Spirit's love to flow through us to help us. It's a similar

thing when we pray. Sometimes we don't know what to say. That's when speaking in tongues can really help us. It's a great gift to have from God!

Rather than allowing our own thoughts to be spoken out, we choose to allow the Holy Spirit's thoughts to be on our lips. But don't worry – the Holy Spirit won't ever force us to say anything against our will. It's completely our choice, but He loves it when His life is allowed to flow through us like this.

From Bible book Acts onward there are loads of stories about people speaking in tongues, so it's not something that's reserved for just a few special people.

This supernatural ability is available to *all of us*. If you don't believe me, grab your Bible and check out 1 Corinthians 14:5.

INSIDE INFORMATION

There's a great bit in the Bible which says that with God, all things are possible! This next Bible story is all about the Holy Spirit helping somebody to do something impossible. And that person was none other than Jesus.

The story begins with Jesus in a place called Galilee, where He'd begun to build His team of disciples.

These were the men who He would train up to help Him – and what a motley bunch they were! Completely ordinary, the lot of them. One of them was a man called Philip, and he didn't take long to work out that Jesus was pretty special. Here's what Philip told his friend Nathaniel.

'We have found the one whom Moses wrote about... He is Jesus son of Joseph, from Nazareth.'

To be honest, Nathaniel wasn't convinced. 'Can anything good come from Nazareth?' he asked.

Philip wasn't going to give up on his friend quite so easily, and persuaded Nathaniel to meet Jesus so he could check Him out for himself.

Off they went to find Jesus, and as the pair approached Him, Jesus stunned Nathaniel with these words:

'Here is a real Israelite; there is nothing false in him!'

Nathaniel was rather taken aback! How did this Jesus know anything about him? They'd never met before.

Good question!

Here's how. The Holy Spirit had given Jesus personal information about Nathaniel, including the fact that he'd just been under a fig tree before coming over to meet Jesus. Very specific indeed!

The Bible calls this a 'word of knowledge', and the Holy Spirit gives them to people – not to freak them out, but to show that God knows them and cares for them. Their purpose is to draw people into a relationship with the living and loving God!

To find out how Nathaniel responded to this word of knowledge go to John 1:49.

BOUNCING BABY

I n the Old Testament part of the Bible you can read about the Holy Spirit coming upon people for a reason or for a season. Not so with the star of this next Bible story, featured in the New Testament. His name was John and he was the person God had chosen to introduce the people of Israel to Jesus.

You'll probably know him by the name John the Baptist, but 'The Baptist' wasn't his surname, just his job title! In case you hadn't guessed, John baptised people. You can find out about John in the New Testament part of the Bible, and his claim to fame is being the first person to have the Holy Spirit come upon him and *remain* upon him.

Even before John's birth it was obvious he was special in God's sight. An angel had appeared to his dad (Zechariah) and informed him that not only would he have a son, but that John (the name God gave him) would be filled with the Holy Spirit while he was still in his mother Elizabeth's womb.

For your information, Elizabeth was a relative of Jesus' mum, Mary. When Mary discovered she was pregnant she raced over to tell Elizabeth the good news. The Bible says that when Mary arrived at Elizabeth's house, the baby inside

Elizabeth leapt. It was as if baby John knew that Jesus was in the house and he simply couldn't contain himself! At that moment Elizabeth was filled with the Holy Spirit. Who knows if this is what the angel meant about John having the Holy Spirit before he was born.

Either way, John's life was never going to be the same again! And nor, for that matter, was his mum and dad's. When John was born, Zechariah could hardly contain himself.

Under the inspiration of the Holy Spirit, Zechariah blurted out some amazing stuff about his baby boy.

You can read about it in Luke 1:67-79.

SUPER SAMSON

When it comes to strong men, Samson must be one of the most famous. This hunky hulk pops up in Bible book Judges at a time when the Israelite nation was having a hard time from their near neighbours, the Philistines.

For 40 years they'd suffered under the hands of the Philistines (as a consequence of turning away from God). The Israelites finally came to their senses and turned back to God, so God came to their rescue by sending Samson.

Up until that point, Samson's parents had been childless – but an angel from God showed up to tell them the good news that they were going to have a boy! God also said that their boy was going to be special to Him, so he wasn't to cut his hair, eat certain foods or drink alcohol.

The Bible says that as Samson was growing up the Holy Spirit came upon him to enable him to be the rescuer that Israel needed. With the Holy Spirit's power upon him, Samson gained a reputation for his awesome strength. One time he even killed a lion with his bare hands. Wow!

Another time he wreaked havoc in the fields of the Philistines by capturing 300 foxes, tying their tails together in pairs, attaching a flaming torch to them and then setting them

loose to destroy the enemy's crops. Pretty creative…

The Philistines were beginning to get a bit fed up with Samson's super powers and persuaded the woman he loved, Delilah, to find out the secret of his strength. After a few failed attempts at trying to trick Samson into spilling the beans, he eventually came clean and told Delilah the secret of his super powers: a vow had been made to God that his hair wouldn't be cut.

You guessed it – Delilah blabbed. While Samson was asleep, the Philistines grabbed their chance and cut Samson's luscious locks. With his strength sapped, they bound him and took him away as a prisoner.

Did Samson's supernatural strength ever return? Head to Judges 16:22–31 to find out!

15
GOLDEN GAFFE

Moses features a lot in the Bible. His job was to lead the Israelite nation out of slavery in Egypt to a new land that God had given them to live in. Because the Israelites had made some bad choices, the short journey to Canaan (where they were heading) took a teensy bit longer than God had planned… 40 whole years, to be precise!

Throughout their weary wanderings, God had looked after the Israelites. He'd given them food, He'd given them water and He'd made sure their clothes didn't wear out. You'd think they'd have been extremely grateful, but they weren't.

And to prove my point, on one particular occasion, while Moses was away up a mountain spending some time with God (40 days, in fact) the Israelites did something rather silly. They had a whip-round and collected all the gold rings and earrings they could muster, melted them down and made a gold calf to worship in place of God.

This was a bad move. God was none-too-pleased… and nor, for that matter, was Moses.

On his return, Moses seized the golden calf, ground it to powder, scattered it on the water and forced the people to drink it. Yuck! God then gave the Israelites their marching orders to leave the mountain and head towards Canaan. God informed Moses that He'd had enough of the rebellious Israelites and wouldn't be joining them for the rest of the journey. He'd send an angel to look after them instead.

But Moses was having none of it. To him it was absolutely vital that the Holy Spirit (God's presence) accompanied them.

Why was Moses making such a big thing about the Holy Spirit being with the Israelites? Find Exodus 33:15–16 to discover why.

16
THATAWAY!

One person who crops up a lot in the Bible is a guy called Paul. Not only is he famous for writing some sizeable chunks of the New Testament, he's also renowned for his epic journeys around the Mediterranean region.

It wasn't the case that Paul had the travel bug and couldn't stay in one place for long. The reason Paul hot-footed it everywhere was to tell people about Jesus. Paul was almost unstoppable in wanting to share his story of how Jesus had changed him from being an enemy of the Christian Church to its number one fan.

Over his lifetime Paul made three mahoosive journeys across land and sea, which took him around 16 years in total. As he travelled Paul shared his faith, but also encouraged other Christians and helped start new churches. But it was certainly not all plain sailing! Paul got shipwrecked as well as attacked, beaten and imprisoned.

For now we're going to focus on Paul's second journey, which took him from Israel, around the north of the Mediterranean, all the way to Greece and back again to where he'd started. That hadn't always been the plan. Paul's intention was to go into Asia, but I'll tell you about that in a moment.

About a quarter of the way along his trip, at a place called
Lystra, Paul was joined by a young fella called Timothy, who
became his travelling companion and right-hand man on
his travels. Now, if you've ever seen a sat nav in a car, you'll
probably know that some of them can redirect you to a faster
route when you're about to hit bad traffic. Paul and Timothy
didn't have anything like that in those days, but what they
did have was the Holy Spirit. As the dynamic duo prepared to
enter into Asia, the Holy Spirit redirected them towards where
He wanted them to go.

To find out where the
Holy Spirit *did* want
them to go you'll need
to read Acts 16:8-10.

17

THE BIG BOOK

When you ask some people the question, 'Who wrote the Bible?', the chances are they'll say that it was God. Well, that's sort of true, but not completely. Let me explain.

First off, you need to understand that the Bible was actually written by around forty different people, over a period of approximately 1,500 years. So it didn't all happen at the same time or in the same place. These writers were a right old mix of businessmen, traders, shepherds, fishermen, soldiers, physicians, preachers and kings. People from all walks of life. But as diverse as they were, they all had one thing in common and it was this:

They were all inspired by the Holy Spirit to write what they did.

So, how did the Holy Spirit give them the ideas for what to write down? Now that's a very good question. Well, for starters, it wasn't just God dictating it to them, word for word, shouting words from heaven as they frantically scribbled away. Each of the writers was a person who'd spent time getting to know God in their own special way. So they each had a personal experience of God – and they'd also had a ringside seat in seeing God do some amazing things.

Some of the Bible is history, so they just needed the Holy Spirit's help to remember what had happened and to know what was important to record. Some of the writers were prophets who passed on to people what God was saying. What they wrote down was an accurate record of the messages the Holy Spirit had given them. And some of the writers were given a special understanding of who God is, what He's like and what He requires of us. They wrote down what the Holy Spirit revealed to them.

18
SIMPLE SIMON

We're now heading to a place called Samaria, where you're going to find out about a man who lived there: Simon. Simon had been impressing the inhabitants of the city with his magic – but this magic wasn't just card tricks or pulling rabbits out of hats. This was dark stuff – what the Bible calls 'witchcraft' – and such was Simon's reputation that he had even been given the nickname 'The Great Power'.

All that changed one day when a chap called Philip (aka Fabulously Fast Phil – remember him?!) arrived in Samaria to tell people about Jesus and to do miracles by the power of the Holy Spirit. People were being healed and set free – left, right and centre. Very soon the crowds that had swarmed around Simon were swarming round Philip, hanging on his every word, amazed by what God was doing through him.

Was Simon jealous? Possibly. But what we do know is that he was so bowled over by what he heard and saw of the Holy Spirit's power that he became a Christian himself. Wow!

Word got back to the church in Jerusalem (where Philip had come from) that many people in Samaria were becoming Christians, so they sent two of their top people (Peter and John) to check things out for themselves. When Peter and John arrived from Jerusalem, they very soon realised that although lots of people had become Christians, they'd not actually been filled with the Holy Spirit (which they needed if they were going to do the same sort of things as Philip, Peter and John). So Peter and John placed their hands on the people and prayed for them to be filled with the Holy Spirit. And they were!

Simon was so impressed by seeing people 'zapped' by the Holy Spirit that he asked if he could buy from them the ability to do the same thing.

19
SHOWER POWER

I t's amazing to think that, for the first 30 years of Jesus' life, very few people had a clue that He was the Son of God.

But then, one day, all that changed. Jesus travelled down from Galilee to the River Jordan where a guy called John was baptising people (do you remember our bouncing baby? Well, that's him – all grown up!). Jesus surprised John by asking to be baptised Himself.

John knew who Jesus was, so he was a little taken aback at Jesus' request. Being baptised (being dunked under the water) was a way of showing that you wanted to clean up your life and get right with God. Because Jesus *was* God, He didn't *need* to do this. But Jesus had His reasons, so John duly obliged.

As Jesus came out of the water something extraordinary happened! The Holy Spirit came down from heaven in the appearance of a dove and landed on Jesus.

Next up, a voice from heaven said, 'This is my Son, whom I love; with him I am well pleased.'

Now in case you missed it let me point out to you something surprising that just happened (other than the voice of God booming out from the sky). Although Jesus was (and is) God, we can sometimes forget that He was also human, just like you

and me. When the Holy Spirit had come upon Jesus at His baptism, He was able to begin His work of teaching people about God's love, and demonstrating this by healing them of their sicknesses. Just like we need the Holy Spirit to live the life God has for us, so did Jesus.

To find out one of the first miracles Jesus did with His Holy Spirit power, go to Mark 1:40–42.

COOL SAUL

Allow me to introduce you to a guy called Saul. There were a couple of Sauls in the Bible, but this one's from the Old Testament part. Saul was Israel's very first king (and isn't to be confused with the Saul who pops up in the New Testament, who helpfully changed his name to Paul). Up to this point, Israel had got on rather nicely without a king and relied on God to look after them. But all that was about to change. The Israelites noticed that all the other nations around them had a king, so why not them?

Through the prophet Samuel, God warned the grumbling Israelites that having a king would be a bad move.

God had wanted Israel to be different from all the other nations so that they could be a good example to everyone else, but the Israelites just wanted to be like the rest of them. If a king was what they wanted, a king was what they'd get.

As I said, his name was Saul. He was a handsome chap; tall and very wealthy. Before Saul was crowned king of Israel, there was just the small matter of letting him know that he'd got the job – which Samuel did by pouring a flask of oil over the young man's head. Was Saul more surprised to be covered in oil, or to be told that God had chosen him to be Israel's king?! Who knows?

What we do know is that pouring (or anointing) with oil represented something very special to God.

For Saul to serve God's nation of Israel, he was going to need the Holy Spirit to help him. And that's what the oil was for. It was a sign that God's power and God's authority were on Saul. More on King Saul later!

Anointing people with oil crops up quite a bit in the Bible and it's always for this same reason. Want to read about Saul's big day when he officially became king? Check out 1 Samuel 10:17-24.

21

MIFFED MOSES

Moses was probably Israel's best known leader, and it was the Holy Spirit who gave Moses all the wisdom and strength he needed for the job.

When you consider that, according to the Bible, there were well over two million Israelites, Moses certainly had his work cut out for him. Not only did he act as their leader from the time they left Egypt until just before they entered the land of Canaan (which God had given them), but he was also the middle-man between the Israelites and God. It was tough being their leader, and Moses spent a lot of time talking to God about how things were going – which, more often than not, was not very well…

Even though the Israelites had been held as slaves in Egypt for centuries, it didn't take them long to begin to wish they were back there. Traipsing through the dusty desert wasn't much fun and they didn't mind telling Moses so. As far as they were concerned, the food was much better in Egypt. They were sick and tired of eating the food God had given them and wanted to know why they couldn't have meat for a change. What an ungrateful bunch of moaners!

Their constant complaining was getting Moses down, big time. God could see that things were getting on top of Moses and had a plan. He instructed Moses to fetch 70 of Israel's respected men and take them to the Tabernacle, the special tent the Israelites had made for God. Once there, they waited for God to show up. Sure enough, God came down (in a cloud) and took some of the Holy Spirit that was on Moses and 'zapped' the 70 respected men.

From now on it wouldn't just be Moses who had the Holy Spirit to help him lead the Israelites. The load would be shared, and Moses would no longer need to go it alone.

THIS WAY I DON'T HAVE TO LISTEN TO THEIR MOANING ANYMORE!

To discover something unusual that happened when the Holy Spirit came on the 70 leaders, head to Numbers 11:25.

DOUBLE DOSE

There were two people in the Bible who shared the same claim to fame. One was Enoch, and the other the prophet Elijah. What was it they had in common?

Both of them left the world without dying and were taken straight to heaven! How awesome is that?!

The Bible story we're heading to now is all about the last moments before Elijah made his dramatic exit.

Elijah was well aware what was going to happen to him, and so was Elisha – the man God had chosen to take over from this powerful prophet. And Elijah and Elisha weren't the only ones in the know. Wherever the pair seemed to go, a bunch of prophets popped up to tell Elisha what he didn't really want to hear – that Elijah would soon be gone.

As the pair came to a river, Elijah, cool as a cucumber, rolled up his coat and struck the water with it. Immediately a path opened up through the river, and the two of them walked through on dry ground.

During Elijah's lifetime, the Holy Spirit had enabled him to do some amazing things, so when Elijah asked Elisha what he could give him as a goodbye present, Elisha didn't have to think twice. He boldly asked for a double portion of the Holy

Spirit's power that had been on Elijah. That was some request, but Elijah didn't say no. His one condition was that Elisha could only have it if he saw him when he was taken away.

Tricky, but not impossible.

So Elisha stuck close to Elijah, not letting him out of his sight, not wanting to miss his chance. And suddenly, it happened. Out of nowhere, a flaming chariot, pulled by fiery horses, appeared from the sky. While Elisha gawped wide-eyed at the spectacle, a strong wind whisked Elijah up to heaven before his very eyes!

Did Elisha get his wish? Read 2 Kings 2:13-14 to see.

23

LITTLE CHRISTS

I don't know if you have a nickname, but not everyone likes theirs. Sometimes people use nicknames as insults. That's what happened to the first followers of Jesus, who were at first described as followers of 'the way' before they were ever called Christians. The term 'Christian' actually started out as an insult! It literally meant 'little Christs', because these followers of Jesus were doing the same sort of things that Jesus had done, such as teaching people about God with great authority and healing the sick. So you could say it was also a bit of a compliment, because of how well they were doing.

And what was it that made people say that these first followers of Jesus were just like Him? The answer is *the Holy Spirit*.

As well as having the Holy Spirit to make them kind, loving, generous and all the things that God is, the Holy Spirit also gave them gifts. We're not talking about boxes of chocolates or tickets to see a great band. These were spiritual gifts, which enabled these Christians to do extraordinary things in God's power. For instance, they had the Holy Spirit's power in them to heal sick people, just like Jesus had. The New Testament is full of stories of Jesus' followers healing people in God's power.

They could also prophesy. What's that, you may ask? It's simply saying something encouraging or positive to someone that you believe God wants you to share with them.

Then there's the gift of tongues (which we read about in chapter 11), which is a supernatural language that the Holy Spirit gives people. When it's used in a church, the Holy Spirit will also give someone an interpretation so that everyone can understand what God is saying.

And finally, there are words of knowledge (which get a mention in chapter 12). This is information God gives someone about another person to share with them, so that they know God cares about every detail of their life.

VITAL VISION

When the Church first began (something like two thousand years ago), the only people who attended it were Jews. That's because Jesus was a Jew, and those who led the first church didn't think that God would want Gentiles (non-Jews) anywhere near them.

It wasn't that the Jews were being awkward – it's just that God had given them laws to keep and things to do that made them 'clean' in His sight (as long as they kept these laws). So as far they were concerned, the Gentiles were 'unclean', and they kept them at arm's length. What they hadn't realised was that Jesus' death and resurrection had made it possible for everyone to be made clean in God's sight, without having to obey lots of complicated laws and carry out religious rituals. It was only a little while later that they discovered the error of their ways, and it happened like this.

Peter, one of the church leaders, had a vision from God that changed everything. In the vision, God made it absolutely clear that the Gentiles had as much right to be followers of Jesus as the Jews. This revelation certainly rocked Peter's world, but he wasn't going to disagree with God.

While all this was happening, two servants of a Roman

commander were on their way to Peter to invite him back to meet their master – a man called Cornelius, who believed in God. (An angel had appeared to Cornelius and instructed him to send his servants out like this.)

To cut a long story short, Peter went back with them and told Cornelius and his household about the vision he'd had. While Peter was still speaking, the Holy Spirit came down on Cornelius and the other Gentiles in his house, and they all became Christians then and there!

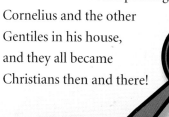

What was the reaction of the church back in Jerusalem to all of this? All is revealed in Acts 11:18.

25
SCARY FOR MARY

I have no idea what time of the year it is as you're reading this book, but we're about to get all Christmassy!

This Bible story involves an angel, a young women called Mary, and of course the Holy Spirit – because that's who this book is about!

The angel went by the name of Gabriel, and it was becoming a busy time for him. A few months earlier, he'd visited the hubby of a relative of Mary to let him know that God was going to give them a son (Zechariah – remember that guy?). And now it was Mary's turn.

She lived in a place called Nazareth (in the land of Israel) and was engaged to be married to a chap called Joseph. But the angel Gabriel was about to turn her world upside down.

One day, while Mary was getting on with the ordinary things of life, Gabriel appeared. The Bible doesn't tell us what Mary's reaction was, but I'd imagine she was gobsmacked. Gabriel's opening lines to Mary were also rather incredible: 'You are truly blessed! The Lord is with you.'

Mary was a bit confused by this. What on earth had an ordinary girl like her done to deserve a greeting like that from an angel of God, and what on earth was he on about?!

Gabriel attempted to put Mary's mind at rest. 'Don't be afraid! God is pleased with you, and you will have a son. His name will be Jesus. He will be great and will be called the Son of God Most High. The Lord God will make Him King, as His ancestor David was. He will rule the people of Israel forever, and His kingdom will never end.'

I'm not sure if what he said made things better or worse, but Mary had a question for the angel.

'How can this happen? I am not married!'

26

CHURCH CHECK-UP

Being a Christian isn't always easy, and in the early days of the Church, Christians were often given a hard time because of their beliefs. One of these Christians had ended up being banished to the island of Patmos, where he ended his days as an old man.

His name was John, and while he was there, the Holy Spirit came upon him powerfully and told him to write a book about the things that God was about to show him. John was then instructed to send the book to the seven churches in Asia. The churches then weren't like churches nowadays. A church wasn't a building but a community of Christians in a town. They might meet in various buildings, but they also might meet in homes or in the open air. The seven churches were in Ephesus, Smyrna, Pergamum, Thyatira, Sardis, Philadelphia, and Laodicea (and yes, some of them are difficult to pronounce!).

So, what sort of things did the Holy Spirit want John to write to these churches?

Before I tell you, it's good to remind ourselves that the Holy Spirit is God, and God always wants the best for us. Often the Holy Spirit just needs to cheer us on with encouragement and advice, but sometimes we need to be reminded that we could behave better. Of course, the Holy Spirit will be right by our side to help us pull our socks up and live the sort of life God expects.

That's the sort of message the Holy Spirit had for those seven churches. For instance, the church in Ephesus was encouraged to keep on going even though things were sometimes a bit tough. They were doing great. On the down side, because of all this, they'd sort of forgotten that important bit about doing it out of their love for God.

Then again, a couple of the churches actually got full marks from the Holy Spirit. So well done them!

You can read about one of these in Revelation 3:7-13.

27

TEMPLE TIME

I f I asked you where God lives, you'd probably tell me that He lives in heaven. And you'd be right. Well, sort of.

Although God does live in heaven, because He's God, He's not like you and me (obviously!). Unlike us, God can be in more than one place at the same time. That's because He's a spirit and not flesh and blood. How God does that is another matter entirely.

In the Old Testament part of the Bible you can read about how God instructed the Israelites to make a tent for Him to live in, so that He could be in the middle of their camp as they moved from place to place.

It was called the Tabernacle, and that's where God's Spirit took up residence.

Israel's second king, David, was keen to build a permanent home for God in their capital city, Jerusalem.

When the Israelites eventually had a land of their own, the Tabernacle was upgraded to a Temple.

But sadly, King David never got to see it. His son Solomon, Israel's next king, got to build this magnificent structure.

In fact, Israel had not one but *three* temples, each replacing the previous one. The first two were destroyed, and the last one

was Herod's Temple, which was around at the time of Jesus.

This was also eventually destroyed by the Romans but God hadn't quite finished with the idea of temples.

Israel's temples weren't an end in themselves, and actually represented God's ultimate plan for each of us.

Although it must have been awesome for the Israelites to have God's presence (His Holy Spirit) nearby, God had something bigger and better up His sleeve. When we become Christians, the Holy Spirit doesn't need to live in a temple made of stone anymore.
He comes to live in us.

To find out what that has to do with temples, head for 1 Corinthians 6:19.

28
SHAKEN, NOT STIRRED

Imagine being arrested for healing a crippled man. It sounds ridiculous, but that's exactly what happened to Peter and John in this Bible story!

The Jewish religious leaders in Jerusalem didn't particularly like them (or, for that matter, anyone who believed that Jesus was the Son of God – which Peter and John did!). They also didn't much like the crowds that Peter and John had attracted when they'd healed the crippled man.

Peter and John had made it perfectly clear that it wasn't their power that had made him well – it was the Holy Spirit who was living in them. But the religious leaders weren't buying all that mumbo jumbo (as far as they were concerned) and had the pair put on trial in front of their religious council.

To be honest, the religious council was rather flummoxed. There was no denying that a miracle had taken place. It was the talk of the city, but the religious leaders were jealous of Peter and John's popularity – or, more to the point, they were jealous of Jesus' popularity.

Something had to be done, so they forbade the troublesome

pair to speak publicly about Jesus. But Peter and John weren't about to be silenced quite so easily.

'Do you think God wants us to obey you or to obey Him? We cannot keep quiet about what we have seen and heard!' was their reply.

The religious leaders were at a loss to know what to do. With no reason to detain them any longer, they released Peter and John (with just a few threats thrown in for good measure).

Peter and John headed back to tell their friends at the church what had happened. Did they take any notice of the threats of the religious leaders? Nope! It actually had the opposite effect on them.

To find out how they responded and what the Holy Spirit did, go to Acts 4:29-31.

29

100% GUARANTEED

lthough God lives in heaven, He doesn't want us to feel like we're a million miles away from Him.

In fact, when we become Christians, God wants us to feel like we're part of His family.

The Bible says that when Adam and Eve (the world's first people) disobeyed God, it spoiled their relationship with Him. All through the Bible you can read about the things God did to get things patched up between Him and us. That's the reason Jesus came to earth – to make that possible. When we put our trust in Jesus as our Lord and Saviour, the gap between us and God disappears and He becomes our Heavenly Father. Amazing!

But because we can't see Father God like we can see a real-life dad, we can sometimes find it difficult to believe that we really do belong to God's family. This is where the Holy Spirit helps us. Not only does the Holy Spirit come to live inside us but His job is also to make us absolutely sure of the fact that we are God's children. God doesn't want us to doubt it for one moment.

In another place in the Bible it says that this is like God adopting us. When a human mum and dad adopt a child, they welcome that child into their home as if they were their own.

Everything they have belongs to their adopted child. That's what being a family is all about. And that's what it's like being part of God's family, too!

30

AN INSIDE JOB

Moses is a guy who features a lot in the Bible, but one of the things he's best known for is the Ten Commandments. God had called him up to the top Mount Sinai, where He gave Moses two slabs of stone. On the slabs, God had written ten laws that He wanted the Israelites to live by. Up until that point, most people had been doing their own thing and living lives that didn't match up to how God wanted them to live. God is good, loving and holy, and His plan was that we would be the same. But unfortunately, things hadn't worked out as planned and people turned their backs on God and did anything they pleased. Most of the time this was the complete opposite of how God wanted them to live.

The Ten Commandments (and other laws) were God's way of reminding people what He expected of them.

God isn't a spoilsport – these laws weren't to make people miserable but to help them live lives that would please God and make them happy. They were good for everyone! But try as they might, the Israelites found it really hard to do the right thing all the time. God was patient with them, and when they said sorry for messing up, He forgave them.

But God knew that unless their hearts were changed they would never make a go of keeping His laws.

How was God going to do that? By putting His Holy Spirit in people. With God's Spirit living inside us, it would be possible to do what the Israelites had found impossible.

31

BEST BUDDIES

You may know this already, but the Holy Spirit is not just a force or a power – He's a person, just like Father God and Jesus are. And because He's a person, the Holy Spirit has feelings, just like you and me. Being God, His feelings aren't up and down like some people's are, but He's still sensitive and He has emotions.

When we understand this about the Holy Spirit, it helps us to realise that He can be our friend and that we can actually have a relationship with Him.

Just like the disciples got to know Jesus really well over the three years that they spent with Him, we too can get to know the Holy Spirit really well. The Holy Spirit loves being our friend, if we'll allow Him to be. Sometimes people keep the Holy Spirit at arm's length because they're worried that He might do something scary or weird. But that couldn't be further from the truth.

The Holy Spirit always wants the best for us, but Bible book Ephesians (chapter four, verse 30) tells us that it's possible to make the Holy Spirit sad. How can we do that? Well, we can do that by ignoring Him. For example, the Holy Spirit might try to stop us saying or doing something bad, but we don't

take any notice of Him and do it anyway. That makes Him sad because He knows that it hurts other people, and that it's not the best way for us to live. Or maybe we never find time in our day to spend with Him. That makes Him sad because He loves hanging out with us.

We wouldn't ignore our other friends, would we? So let's not ignore Him.

Spending time with the Holy Spirit makes Him happy, but did you know it can make us happy as well? Check out Acts 13:52 to read about this for yourself.

32

MEGA MAKEOVER

King Saul pops up more than once in this book (and you might remember some of this story from a bit earlier on). This time I'm going to tell you about the difference that having the Holy Spirit made to him.

We catch up with Saul before he'd actually been made king. All the action takes place in the land of Israel where, at that particular time, the prophet Samuel was God's main man. Samuel had been given the job, by God, to give Israel their first king.

God had handpicked Saul as the man to be king, and Samuel was now on his way to break the news to Saul.

Samuel took a small jar of olive oil and poured it on Saul's head. Then he kissed Saul and told him, 'The Lord has chosen you to be the leader and ruler of his people.'

Samuel then gave Saul a heads-up about what was going to happen to him next, including meeting a bunch of prophets who were prophesying in a town called Gibeah. At that moment, the Holy Spirit was going to fall powerfully on Saul and he'd also start prophesying.

If you're wondering what prophesying is, let me explain. It's simply the Holy Spirit giving you things to say that you then share with other people. God loves letting us know what's on His heart and prophesying is a great way of doing that (more on that later!).

There was one more bit of useful info that Samuel had for Saul – he told him that when the Holy Spirit came upon him, he would be a different person. Really?

Well, obviously he'd still be Saul – but the Holy Spirit was going to give him all the abilities he needed to be Israel's king that he didn't have already.

33

ELYMAS MEETS HIS MATCH

Paul and Barnabas were on their way to the Mediterranean Island of Cyprus to tell people about Jesus. Just for the record, the Bible says that they were also accompanied by a fella called John. Don't want him feeling left out, do we?

This dynamic duo (plus John) had been sent out by the church in a place called Antioch, and on their arrival they wasted no time in making a beeline for the Jewish synagogues in Cyprus to do their stuff. The three of them traipsed to the other side of the island until they reached the city of Paphos.

While they were there, they bumped into (not literally) a man called Bar-Jesus. He also went by the name of Elymas, so that's what we'll call him from now on. Elymas was Jewish (like Paul, Barnabas and John) but he also dabbled in things that he shouldn't have done, such as witchcraft. (Remember Simon, earlier in this book? They'd have probably got on well.) And if that wasn't bad enough, Elymas was also a false prophet, which meant that although he made out his words came from God, they didn't. They were either things he'd made up or things the devil had inspired him to say.

Elymas worked for Sergius Paulus (the governor of Cyprus), who the Bible informs us was very smart (as in intelligent, not that he wore fancy suits every day). Sergius Paulus was smart enough to realise that he needed to listen to what Paul and Barnabas had to say about Jesus. But Elymas had other ideas, and did everything in his power to prevent the governor from having faith in Jesus.

Paul was having none of it. The Holy Spirit came upon Paul in power and gave him the boldness and authority to deal with Elymas' tactics once and for all. Paul didn't mince his words.

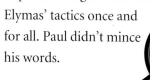

To find out what he said to Elymas, look up Acts 13:9–12.

34

SIMEON'S SURPRISE

When Jesus was born, you'd think that there was hardly anybody left up in heaven. Down here on earth there were angels appearing all over the place – in dreams or face-to-face – getting people ready for Jesus' arrival! (There was also a chap called Simeon who'd had a heads-up from the Holy Spirit about Jesus' birth, but we'll get to him in a moment.)

For example, there was Mary, Jesus' mum, who had a visit from an angel to tell her that Jesus was on the way. Next up, her future hubby, Joseph, had a dream where an angel appeared to him to say that it was still OK to marry his pregnant wife-to-be. And not forgetting those surprised shepherds in the Christmas story, who were minding their own business when a whole sky-full of angels showed up to announce the birth of Jesus! It was pretty obvious from these angelic appearances that God wanted enough people to know that His one and only Son, Jesus, was about to come to the world.

The drama didn't stop when Jesus was born. There was more to come, but this time it would be the Holy Spirit who was centre-stage. Eight days after Jesus' birth, Jesus' mum and dad took Him to the Temple in Jerusalem to offer a sacrifice to God as their law required. The Jewish law said that parents

had to give a sacrifice of at least a pair of doves or two young pigeons. So that's what Mary and Joseph did. And that's where Simeon comes in.

Simeon loved God, and he knew from the Jewish scriptures that one day God would send a Messiah to Israel, someone from God who would rescue them. The Holy Spirit had told Simeon that he wouldn't die until this had happened. And now that day had finally arrived.

Simeon, prompted by the Holy Spirit, was on his way to the Temple. Mary and Joseph must have been a little taken aback when Simeon took the baby Jesus in his arms and made a speech about Him, inspired by the Holy Spirit.

To find out what Simeon said, go to Luke 2:29-32.

35

MIRACLE MAN

Our next Bible story is about a crippled man who spent his days begging outside Jerusalem's Temple.

Little did he know that this was going to be the day that changed his life forever.

Peter and John, a couple of Christians from that city, were on their way to the Temple and happened to pass by the poor beggar on this particular day. Perhaps they had passed by him every time they went to the Temple, but this time things were going to be different.

As Peter and John walked past, the lame man asked them for money. The pair stopped in their tracks, caught his gaze and said, 'Look up at us!'

The beggar probably hadn't a clue why they said that, but he dutifully obeyed. Maybe he was expecting to receive some much-needed money to buy food, but that's not what happened.

Peter quashed that notion with these words:

'I have no money at all, but I give you what I have: in the name of Jesus Christ of Nazareth I order you to get up and walk!'

Well, that certainly wasn't what the beggar had been anticipating!

Then, without warning, Peter grabbed the man's right hand and pulled him to his feet. What was Peter up to? Had he made a big mistake? Nothing of the sort! At that very moment the man's feet and ankles became strong, and he leapt up and began walking around. It was a miracle!

You see, Peter and John knew full well that in their own ability they couldn't heal anybody. But with the Holy Spirit living inside them they had the same power that Jesus had to make sick people well. This powerful pair knew what they had, and they used it.

I WASN'T EXPECTING THAT!

To read how the people of the city reacted to this miracle, head to Acts 3:8–10.

36 ✦ THREE IN ONE

Throughout this book, I've been talking about Father God, Jesus and the Holy Spirit. For instance, at the beginning of the Bible we're told that it was Father God who created everything (although, for the record, Jesus and the Holy Spirit also had a big part to play in it).

Fast forward a few thousand years to the time of Jesus. It soon became obvious to many people at the time that Jesus wasn't just a good man or a prophet of God. He *was* God.

One of Jesus' disciples, called Thomas, became so convinced that Jesus was God that he couldn't contain himself.

'My Lord and my God!' was how he put it.

And then of course there's the star of this book, the Holy Spirit. Once again the Bible makes it clear in loads of places that He is most definitely God. (Not forgetting that the Holy Spirit also gets the credit for being the author of the Bible!) So you could be forgiven for coming to the conclusion that there are actually three Gods... but as you're about to find out, that's not the case.

Here's a Bible bit to back me up on this:

'Hear, O Israel: The LORD our God, the LORD is one.'
(You can find that in Deuteronomy 6:4.)

What we've got is one God, but He exists as three persons: Father, Son (Jesus) and Holy Spirit. Each person is fully God, while at the same time being an individual.

As human beings, we each of us only ever exist as one person. You're you, and I'm me. But the one God is three persons. How mind-bogglingly awesome is that?! (For your info, sometimes people call this the Trinity or the Godhead.)

OK, so I'll admit that it can all sound a little bit confusing – but you have to remember that God is God, and we're not.

There are some things that we simply can't get our heads around completely and that's just the way it is.

To find out how you can have the Holy Spirit in your life, head to Luke 11:13.

37

THAT'S MY BOY!

I magine you were going to meet someone who you'd never met before, but you hadn't a clue what they looked like. The best way around that problem would be to tell them something about you that would identify you, right? For instance, you might have bright red hair, or be wearing a stripy shirt. Well, that's sort of what happened when Jesus came from heaven to earth (except it wasn't a bright red hair or stripy shirt thing).

God was sending His one and only Son to rescue us, but there was just one teeny tiny problem. Jesus wasn't going to look like God when He showed up. Jesus was going to look like an ordinary human being.

But God had thought this one through, and dropped plenty of clues as to how people would spot Jesus when He arrived.

The Old Testament part of the Bible has loads of prophecies telling people where Jesus would be born, the sort of life He'd live, and even the circumstances of His death. In fact, there were well over three hundred of them, just so that people wouldn't miss Him. And yes, you guessed it – it was the Holy Spirit who inspired these prophecies about Jesus.

But it wasn't just the things that happened to Jesus that helped mark Him out as God's Son. In Isaiah chapter 11, we are told that the Holy Spirit also got the job of pointing out who Jesus was by what He would say and the way He would do things. How did He do that? The Holy Spirit gave Jesus such wisdom, understanding and knowledge that people would be in no doubt that this man was not like anyone else.

38

IS ANYBODY THERE?

ave you ever wanted to hear God speak to you? You're not alone. Many people would love to hear God say something to them, but the trouble is they're worried that they might not recognise His voice when He does. While it's true that God does speak to some people so that they can hear Him with their ears, that doesn't happen all that often. God actually speaks to us in lots of different ways, and this is the job of the Holy Spirit.

I've already mentioned in this book that it was the Holy Spirit who inspired the writers of the Bible to write what they did. But did you know that God can speak to us *through* the Bible? Well, He can – and I'll tell you how.

You might have heard people calling the Bible the 'Word of God'. That's because it contains the things God has said! So we can read the Bible and know that the words we read are the things God wants us to know about Him and are the things He wants to say to us.

There's more, though.

In Bible book Hebrews (chapter 4, verse 12) it tells us that the Word of God is *alive* and *active*. The Bible is full of life? That sounds freaky! But fear not! You don't have to worry that it might leap out of your hand at any minute. That's not what it means.

What it actually means is that because the Holy Spirit is the author of the Bible, and because He is still with us, when we read the Bible He can highlight bits of it to us and make it seem as if God has written them just for us. It's as if God is speaking to us directly through the Bible.

So what do you do when God has spoken to you through the Bible? Head to James 1:22 to find out.

39

GOOD NEWS

I don't know about you, but I like learning new words. There's a word you may not have heard before, which the Bible uses to describe everything that Jesus has done for us. The word is 'gospel', and it literally means 'good news'. That's because Jesus taking the punishment for the bad stuff in our lives is just that – good news!

When you read the Bible, you could be forgiven for thinking it's mostly bad news with so much fighting and bickering going on. But the thing about the Bible is that it doesn't cover up the bad stuff that people do – it tells us how it was, warts and all.

When we read about God punishing people, particularly in the Old Testament, it wasn't because He was mad at them. God has never stopped being loving, kind and good, but sometimes He had to step in to protect people from themselves or from those who wanted to do them harm. God could have given up on the human race for turning their backs on Him and for all their wickedness, but He didn't. God has always wanted the very best for us, and the Bible is all about how He made it possible for us to be His friends again. The good news is that Jesus did this for us, but there's more. God's plan was for us to have His Holy Spirit living inside us so that He could be really close to us. The bad stuff in our lives made that impossible, but Jesus changed all that. Thousands of years ago God spoke about this through a prophet called Joel, to announce that one day, the Holy Spirit would be able to live in everyone, if they wanted. Young or old. Male or female. Everyone could have the Holy Spirit.

40
DREAM ON

There are plenty of stories in the Bible about God speaking to people. Sometimes God sends an angel to do the talking, sometimes He shows up Himself, and sometimes God speaks to people in dreams.

These aren't the only ways that God speaks to us, but this next Bible story features a young fella that you've probably heard of – and who had more than his fair share of dreams from God!

His name was Joseph, and he had his first dream from God when he was just 17 years old. The dreams Joseph had weren't any old dreams. They were God's way of giving him a heads-up of the plans He had for his life, and how Joseph would one day be the head of his family.

But Joseph had to wait another 13 years to see these dreams fulfilled. Having been sold into slavery in Egypt by his jealous brothers, and then thrown into prison for something he didn't do, Joseph might have thought that his dreams from God would never come true! But God always keeps His promises, and at the age of 30, Joseph suddenly got the job of being second-in-command to the Pharaoh of Egypt.

How did this happen? To cut a long story short, Pharaoh had a couple of dreams of his own, God told Joseph what they

meant and Pharaoh rewarded him with the job as his number two. You'll be pleased to know that Joseph was reunited with his long-lost family and they patched up their differences.

And if you hadn't worked it out already, it was the Holy Spirit who had given Joseph these incredible dreams as well as giving him the ability to interpret Pharaoh's dreams.

Perhaps God will speak to you in a dream as well. You just never know!

To read about another couple of dreams that Joseph interpreted with the Holy Spirit's help, go to Genesis 40:1-23.

41
LIAR, LIAR

The world's first church was a very generous church indeed. It met in Jerusalem and everyone was more than happy to share what they had with everyone else. A man named Barnabas even went so far as to sell a house he had, and then gave the proceeds to the church so that nobody would lack anything. How kind was that?!

The church's generosity was contagious, and another couple from the church decided to do the same as Barnabas. Their names were Ananias and Sapphira, but they weren't quite as honest as Barnabas. The devious duo conspired to deceive the church and keep back some of the money from the sale of their property for themselves. This was a bad move, as you will soon discover.

When Ananias brought the money (minus their secret cut of it) to Peter, one of the leaders of the church, he thought he'd get away with it. But Peter had some inside information from the Holy Spirit that there had been dirty dealings going on, and that Ananias was telling a whopper of a fib.

Peter was not a happy bunny, and didn't hold back from telling Ananias what he thought of him.

'Why has Satan made you keep back some of the money

from the sale of the property? Why have you lied to the Holy Spirit? The property was yours before you sold it, and even after you sold it, the money was still yours. What made you do such a thing? You didn't lie to people. You lied to God!'

Immediately Ananias dropped dead, right in front of Peter!

The Bible doesn't explain why lying to the Holy Spirit caused him to die, but it does show us how keen God was not to let deception spoil the Church.

You might remember that Adam and Eve were deceived by Satan in the Garden of Eden, and how that spoiled our friendship with God. No way was Satan, known as the Deceiver, going to get a second crack at the whip.

Want to find out what became of Sapphira? Scoot over to Acts 5:7-10.

42

DOUBLE MEANING

Who likes being told they've done something wrong? I certainly don't.

Being praised for doing a good deed or getting a pat on the back for getting ten out of ten in a test makes you feel on top of the world, doesn't it? But being in someone's bad books is another story altogether. When we've messed up, most of us feel ashamed, guilty and regret what we did.

In the old days, someone who was caught doing wrong by committing a crime was called a 'convict'. It simply means that those who were charging them with an offence were convinced that they were in the wrong. The police would arrest them, they'd be sent to court for a trial and if found guilty they would be convicted of their crime. With that, the criminal would be sentenced to whatever punishment the judge decided was appropriate. So, being 'convicted' is probably not something we take kindly to.

Before Jesus returned to heaven, He had something to say about the Holy Spirit that might have surprised His disciples. He said that after He'd gone, the Holy Spirit would 'convict' people about the wrong stuff they do.

Hang on a minute… you're probably thinking. *Isn't the Holy Spirit meant to be kind to us and to help us? Pointing out what we've done wrong doesn't seem to fit in with that.*

You're totally right. That's not what this Bible bit means at all. It's not about making us feel like we're no good, but about convincing us to put our trust in Jesus so He can get rid of all that bad stuff for us. How great is that?! So being convicted can sometimes be a good thing after all!

43
HERE COMES THE BRIDE

One thing you'll have discovered about the Holy Spirit, by reading this book, is that He is at work all through the Bible. He's there at the beginning of time, He's there right through the Old Testament, He's there when Jesus is conceived, He's there at the start of the Church and He shows up right at the end of the Bible when God brings history to a close.

Yes, you did hear me right. Not only did God create the world and the universe in which it snuggly sits, but the Bible tells of a time when God will one day wrap things up and do something new.

God's plan is to give the universe a wonderful makeover and get rid of all the bad stuff, once and for all, so that we can enjoy life to the full and enjoy being with God.

Now that sounds good to me!

As part of this whole process there's going to be a wedding, and it's something Jesus has been looking forward to for a long time – the reason being that it's Jesus who is getting married! He didn't have a wife while He lived on earth but He'll have one in the future.

Confused? Let me explain.

There will come a time when everyone who loves Jesus will get to be with Him forever. The Bible says that this is like a man and a woman getting ready for their wedding day. To start off with, they're apart – but one day they'll be together *always*.

When the Bible talks about this great wedding, Jesus is the Bridegroom and the Church will be His Bride. Now that might sound tricky to get your head around, but that's what the Bible says! And here's where the Holy Spirit comes in. It's the Holy Spirit (along with Jesus) who sends out the invites.

Is this for real? Find out by looking up Revelation 22:17.

44

GLORY CLOUD

I f you hadn't figured it out already from this book, God likes being with us. He created us to be like Him in so many ways, so hanging out with us is always a priority for God. Although God lives in heaven, His Holy Spirit is present with us on the earth to make this happen.

One of Israel's kings called David went so far as to say, 'Where shall I go from your Spirit? Or where shall I flee from your presence?' In fact, when the Bible talks about the Holy Spirit being with us it actually calls it His 'presence', because He is present. Adam and Eve (the world's first people) enjoyed the presence of God in the Garden of Eden.

God's presence was with the Israelites as they travelled towards the land He had given them to live in. By day the Holy Spirit led them in the form of a pillar of cloud. By night He led them in the form of a pillar of fire. As they went on their journey, the Israelites were carrying with them a rather special, ornate box called the Ark of the Covenant, which represented God being with them. The ark (the box, not Noah's big boat!) was not just a symbol of God's presence. God's presence was actually *upon* this ark box.

In time, the Israelites even made a tent in which to house

the ark. Not only was this special tent (called the Tabernacle) made according to God's instructions, but the way the ark was to be approached was also set down by God.

When the Tabernacle was finally completed, Moses (the Israelites' leader) was in for a bit of a surprise. He was about to experience the Holy Spirit's presence in a spectacular way. Read all about it in Exodus 40:34-38.

45
SUPER SERVERS

What do you think of when I say the word 'Christian'?
Do you think of someone who goes to church once a
week, on a Sunday? If so, that's not what Jesus intended
for us to think about people who belong to His Church.

Back in the early days of the Church, being a Christian was an
'all or nothing' sort of thing. As well as being 100% committed
to God, these first Christians allowed the Holy Spirit into every
part of their life, not just Sundays. For them it wasn't enough
to just *tell* people about Jesus – they wanted people to have an
experience of Him. Whether that was healing a person in the
Holy Spirit's power, or speaking some encouraging words from
God to someone, every day was a church day.

So when the leaders of this first church found themselves
getting bogged down by the day-to-day stuff of leading the
church, they figured that it was time to change the way they
did things. Up until that point, the church had a dozen leaders
(called apostles) who, with the exception of one, were Jesus'
disciples when He was on earth. The church they led provided
food for those in need, but a dispute had arisen among them
about some widows who were getting overlooked in the daily
distribution of food.

Something had to be done, but the apostles were keen not to get caught up spending their time serving out food when they should be preaching about Jesus. They hit upon the idea of asking the church to pick seven men to take on the task of giving out the food.

You might think that a mundane job such as that wouldn't require anything particularly spiritual of the people chosen, but think again. As I said, this church made sure that the Holy Spirit was involved in absolutely everything, including something as practical as doling out food.

You can read about what special qualifications these men needed in Acts 6:3-6.

46

BALAAM BERATED

The Israelite nation were journeying towards the land of Canaan and had moved into the territory of King Balak of Moab. The king had heard how the Israelites had defeated the Amorite army, and now it looked like he and his people were next for the chop. He came up with a sneaky plan to ask a prophet called Balaam to pronounce a curse on the Israelites. That ought to stop them in their tracks!

Although Balaam was a prophet of God, his heart had turned bad. That made him perfect for Balak's devious scheme. The cunning king dispatched messengers to Balaam, armed with a stash of cash to bribe him to curse Israel. But when the messengers showed up, God told Balaam to send them packing.

King Balak wasn't one to be put off quite so easily, and sent more messengers to do his dirty work. Balaam knew that he shouldn't curse the Israelites, but he kept the men waiting overnight just in case God changed His mind.

God obviously knew that Balaam would have grabbed the money with both hands if He hadn't said not to, so He told Balaam to go with the messengers. It seemed that God was giving Balaam the opportunity to decide if he wanted to do the right thing or not.

The next morning, Balaam saddled up his donkey and left with the Moabite messengers. God was so cross He sent an angel to stop his wickedness. Balaam was oblivious to the angel, but the donkey could see him as clear as anything and took a detour away from the angel, into a nearby field. Balaam beat the donkey with a stick until he got back on the road.

Next up, the angel stood in a narrow path with a stone wall on each side. When the donkey saw the angel, it walked so close to one of the walls that Balaam's foot scraped against the wall. Balaam beat the donkey again.

Once again the angel tried to bar Balaam's way, and this time he stood in a spot so narrow that there was no room for the donkey to go around. So it just lay down! Balaam was furious and smacked the donkey with a stick.

This is where the Holy Spirit comes in. He was going to give Balaam a right old telling off, but His mouthpiece was not what you'd have expected.

BALAAM IS MAKING AN ASS OF ME.

To find out who the Holy Spirit used to tell Balaam off, go to Numbers 22:22–35.

47

NEW NICK

The nation of Israel has always been special in God's eyes. They had been handpicked by Him to show the rest of the world what He was like. It wasn't because they were better than everyone else; this was just the way God chose to do it.

Along the way, God had given the Jewish people (which was how the Israelites were also known) laws that He commanded them to live by. The religious leaders' job was to help the Jews keep these laws. When Jesus came onto the scene, many of the religious leaders of His day refused to accept that He was the Messiah (a special person sent by God) their scriptures had told them to expect. (Like we said earlier – Jesus didn't look all that much like God!)

But not all of the religious leaders rejected Jesus. Some of them could see that He was more than just a man, and kept an open mind on the matter. It was dangerous and unwise for these people to admit this in public, so they kept their thoughts and conversations in the shadows.

One of them was a guy called Nicodemus, who the Bible describes as a 'ruler of the Jews', so he was a top bod among the religious leaders. Nicodemus wanted to meet with Jesus and, under cover of darkness, he came to Him.

Nicodemus told Jesus he knew God had sent Him to teach them, and that He wouldn't have been able to do all the miracles He'd done if God hadn't been with Him. Jesus' reply was somewhat surprising. Rather than picking up on what Nicodemus had said, Jesus told him that the only way he could see the kingdom of God was if he was 'born again'. Nicodemus was more than a little perplexed! What on earth did Jesus mean by that?

Elsewhere in this book there's a story about how God made the first man out of dirt, and then breathed his Spirit into him so that Adam came to life. When Jesus was conceived in His mum's tum, it was the Spirit of God who gave Jesus life.

Jesus was explaining to Nicodemus that this is also the same way someone is born into God's family. Discover how in John 3:4-6.

48

THE BIG SEND-OFF

This next Bible story stars Saul and Barnabas, who were key players in the Church just under a couple of thousand years ago.

Saul (who later changed his name to Paul) had started out as an enemy of the Church, but had ended up as one of its main men! Not only did Paul write big chunks of the New Testament part of the Bible, but he was also a bit of a keen traveller – and was forever on the go, telling people about Jesus.

Barnabas, on the other hand, was a bit of an all-round good guy. Not only had he sold some land he owned and given the money to the church, but he must have also been a great person to have around because he got the nickname 'son of encouragement'.

By the time we catch up with these two it was many years since Jesus had returned to heaven, and by then there were loads of churches dotted all around the Mediterranean region. One of these was in a place called Antioch (which is now modern-day Turkey). What's any of this got to do with the Holy Spirit? You're about to find out!

While the church were worshipping God, the Holy Spirit told them to appoint Paul and Barnabas to go and do the

work that He had lined up for them. After praying about it, they placed their hands on Paul and Barnabas (to show that they had been appointed to do this work) and then everyone sent them on their way.

What we can learn from this is that if anyone wants to do stuff for God, it's important they get the Holy Spirit's thumbs-up that this is what He wants them to do, just like Paul and Barnabas did.

If you go to Acts 13:4-12 you can find out where this dynamic duo went to first.

49
GOD'S MOUTHPIECES

I n this book I've mentioned prophets or prophecies a few times, but it would be good to fill you in with a bit more info about what they are and how they work. Put simply, a prophecy is something that is spoken on behalf of God, and a prophet is the person who often speaks it. I say 'often', because anyone can actually prophesy – but more on that shortly.

Prophecy is just one way in which God speaks to people. How it works is that the prophet (somebody God has chosen to be His messenger) listens out for what God is saying. The Holy Spirit will speak to their spirit, they'll mull it over in their head until they think they've understood what God is saying, and then they'll write it down or speak it out to whoever the message is directed at.

Sometimes they can be quite serious messages. Perhaps God is wanting a nation to turn from their wicked ways; perhaps a person needs to make some important decisions, or to know what God expects of them.

All through the Old Testament, God was speaking to the Israelites through a whole heap of prophets, for a variety of reasons. These included keeping them on the straight and narrow as well as getting them ready for Jesus coming

to the earth. All in all, these prophecies were a mixture of good news and bad news.

Prophets continued to pop up in the New Testament, but one thing you read a lot more about is what the Bible calls 'the gift of prophecy'.

This is something every Christian is expected to use, but it's nothing to be worried about. When we become a Christian and are filled with the Holy Spirit we can hear from God for ourselves, and use the gift of prophecy to speak words that encourage people and make them feel better. These words that the Holy Spirit gives us help people to realise how much God loves them and cares for them.

If you want to be absolutely convinced that prophesying is for everyone, go to 1 Corinthians 14:5.

IN A NUTSHELL

As you will have discovered by reading this book, the Holy Spirit is involved in everything that God does.

So, as we come to the end, let's do a quick recap of who the Holy Spirit is.

First up, the Holy Spirit *is* God. Although there's only one God, He's three persons – one of whom is the Holy Spirit (the other two being Father God and Jesus). The Holy Spirit hovered over the world at the beginning of time, and brought to life everything that God had in His mind to create. The Holy Spirit then gave life to Adam, the world's first man. All through the Old Testament part of the Bible, the Holy Spirit inspired prophets to speak out what God wanted them to say. When God kick-started the nation of Israel it was the Holy Spirit who looked after them and lived among them. It was the Holy Spirit who overshadowed Mary (Jesus' mum) and brought Jesus into the world. Before Jesus began His mission of telling people about God and healing the sick, the Holy Spirit came on Him to give Him all the power that He'd need.

When someone becomes a Christian (by making Jesus number one in their life) it's the Holy Spirit who comes to live in them to make this real to them.

The Holy Spirit helps Christians to be more like Jesus – loving, kind, generous, forgiving and loads more!

As I said way back in the intro, sometimes it feels that we've been zapped when the Holy Spirit comes upon us but, as you'll have gathered, there is so much more to Him than just a zappy feeling.

And finally, one more thing that the Holy Spirit does: He draws people into a friendship with Jesus. If that's something you've never had and would like, here's a prayer you can pray:

'Dear God, I know I have messed up. I'm sorry for all the wrong things I've done. Jesus, I know that You are God's Son, and that You died for me – so please wash my sins away. Come and live in my heart forever and fill me with your Holy Spirit. Amen.'

Get into God's Word.
Every day.

FOR AGES 7–11

Join the Topz Gang as they explore the Bible through daily Bible readings, puzzles, cartoons and prayers!

FOR AGES 11–14

Read a bit of the Bible every day, explore lots of stuff about you and God – and crack puzzles along the way!

Available as annual subscriptions or single issues, published every two months.

To purchase, go to **www.cwr.org.uk**
or call **01252 784700** or visit a Christian bookshop.

MEET PROFESSOR BUMBLEBRAIN

Uncover mind-boggling facts about God and His Word with brilliant and barmy Bible buff Professor Bumblebrain. With colourful cartoons and (ahem) 'hilarious' jokes, these books address some really big questions!

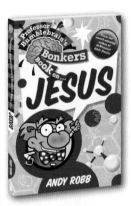

BY ANDY ROBB

PAYING TH

CW00862716

Contents

Badger
LEARNING

Characters

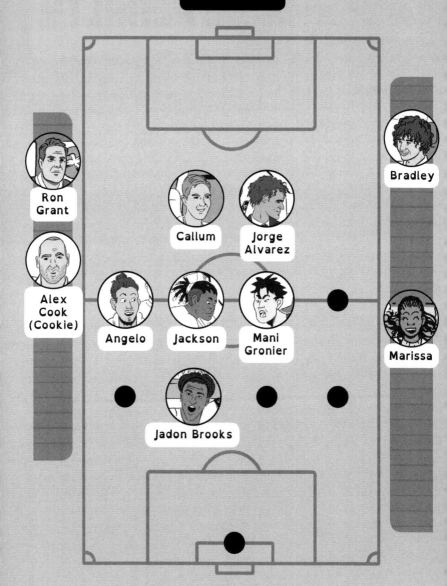

Ron Grant

Alex Cook (Cookie)

Callum

Jorge Alvarez

Angelo

Jackson

Mani Gronier

Jadon Brooks

Bradley

Marissa

Ballon d'Or: an annual football award for the best performing male footballer

converted: to use the chance of a penalty and turn it into a goal

crossed: a medium or long-range pass from the wide area of the field to the centre

digs: housing

inswinger: a free kick or corner that bends in towards the goal

onside: two players from the opposing team are between the attacking player and the goal

outplaying: to be better in skill and technique than the opposing player

pinpoint cross: a pass or shot that goes exactly where the player wants it to go

sitting deep: to have most players positioned closer to their own goal rather than the oppositions

toe-poked: a hard kick[5] to the ball with the

CHAPTER ONE

"Hey, ball boy! How's it going?"

Jackson Mbemba's heart sank. He'd just been home to collect some clean clothes and was on his way off the estate when he met Blake, gang leader and all-round troublemaker.

Blake and his gang were always causing problems. They threatened, they bullied, they stole. They were criminals. One of the main reasons that Jackson wanted to make it as a footballer was to get his family away from the estate and Blake's gang.

Jackson's parents had come to the UK as refugees from Africa. His dad's life had been in danger because he had spoken out against the government. Jackson wanted more than anything for his dad to have an easy life.

Jackson wasn't scared of Blake and he'd told him so, but many others were.

Blake had mostly left Jackson and his family alone, and Jackson really wanted it to stay that way.

Jackson only came back to the estate on Sundays now. The rest of the week he stayed in a house nearer the Stanford ground. He didn't miss seeing Blake, that's for sure. But now, here he was, with his sneery grin and his empty, black-hole eyes.

"I'm fine," Jackson responded at last. He moved to go.

Blake blocked him. "Hey, chill, man. What's the hurry? We've got things to talk about."

Jackson shook his head. "I don't think so."

Blake's sneery grin grew wider. "That's not friendly, bro."

Jackson stood and looked Blake in the eye. "What do you want?"

Blake held out his hands in a mock plea.
"Just a bit of information."

Jackson had expected this. He knew Blake's gang was responsible for robberies on the estate, and now that Jackson was in the Stanford first team, Blake saw an opportunity. He wanted Jackson to give him information about other players — where they lived, what cars they drove and when their houses would be empty. He said Jackson owed him for keeping his family safe.

Jackson laughed, "Keeping them safe? You're the last person I'd trust to do that."

"This estate can be a dangerous place, bro..." Blake threatened.

He was still grinning, but the menace in his words was clear.

Jackson put down his bag of clothes and took a step forwards.

"I don't want anything to do with your dirty business, Blake," he hissed. He pointed a finger at the gang leader. "Stay away from my family."

"Or?" Blake asked.

"Or you'll have to answer to me," replied Jackson.

"Oooh, I'm scared," Blake mocked. "Jackson the boy wonder football star is going to come after me."

Jackson balled his fists. He wanted to punch the sleazy gang leader, but he knew it was a bad idea.

Be strong, stand up for yourself, his dad had always said, *but don't throw the first punch.*

"You should be scared, Blake," he warned.

Then he picked up his bag, turned and walked away. His heart was thumping.

Jackson was proud that he'd stood up to Blake, but he was worried too. What if his words had put his family in danger?

CHAPTER TWO

When Jackson got back to his digs, Mrs Earls had a surprise for him. His teenage teammates, Callum Cooper and Angelo Walker, were moving in to join him. Like Jackson, they had been promoted from the Under-21s to the First Team squad for the Cathay Cup, an international pre-season tournament.

Stanford had drawn their opening match with Sevilla one-all. There were four teams in each group and the winner went through to the final. The other game in the group, between Porto and AC Milan, had also ended in a draw. Stanford's next match, tomorrow, was against Porto.

Ron Grant had decided that he wanted all three of his young players in digs during the tournament so that Mrs Earls could keep an eye on them.

Jackson was happy. Having his friends around would be a good distraction from worrying about Blake and his gang. He was feeling anxious about his younger sister, Marissa. She played for the Stanford women's team and they had a big match at the weekend against Chelsea. It was going to be a special day for Marissa, and Jackson didn't want Blake doing anything to spoil it.

Callum and Angelo brought their stuff with them after training. They had a suitcase each, plus a bag filled with all their football kit.

Mrs Earls welcomed them and told them the house rules. They had to be in by 6pm and ready for dinner at 6.30pm. They had to take it in turns to wash and dry the dishes. They had to be in bed with the lights out by 10pm, or else. Breakfast was at 7.30am sharp. And lastly, they were to address her as 'ma'am'.

"Is that clear?" said Mrs Earls.

"Yes, ma'am," the three young footballers replied.

Callum and Angelo looked like they were regretting their move but Jackson reassured them. He was used to Mrs Earls and her ways. She was strict, but she was kind too — and a great cook. Hearing that cheered Callum and Angelo up a lot!

After a delicious dinner, they spent the evening chatting and then playing FIFA on Angelo's Xbox. They made sure that they were in bed by 10pm.

Tomorrow was going to be a big day.

CHAPTER THREE

Jackson was delighted to find out that he'd kept his place in the team. Angelo was in the starting line-up too, while Callum was on the bench again. He'd get his chance though, Jackson was sure of it. Callum had played really well in their last match against Sevilla.

Grant had made a couple of changes — the most significant for Jackson was the return of Mani Gronier. The club had suspended him for the first match for causing trouble in training. He had badly fouled Jackson who was outplaying him in a practice match.

Jackson hadn't spoken to Gronier since then, and he wasn't sure how Gronier would act towards him. But, to Jackson's relief, he seemed okay.

The Porto game was very much one of two halves. In the first half, Porto had the edge and should have been ahead, but they wasted several chances. In the second half, after another angry team talk from Ron Grant, Stanford took charge.

Jackson and Gronier started to blend better, the Frenchman sitting deep and allowing Jackson to push forwards. Callum replaced veteran striker, Jorge Alvarez, and the attack looked sharper and faster.

Five minutes into the second half, Stanford took the lead. Jackson broke up a Porto attack and fed the ball to Gronier. His long ball out to the wing found Angelo, whose clever footwork took him past the Porto full back. He crossed to the far post where Reegan Keller rose, unchallenged, to score.

After that, it was all Stanford. Porto seemed worn out. Angelo won a penalty that Mani Gronier coolly converted, then Jackson and Callum set up Reegan Keller for his second goal.

Finally, just before the end of the game, Callum got onto the score sheet for the first time. A fifty-yard pass from Gronier found Callum just onside as he broke through the middle and behind the Porto defence. As the keeper came out, Callum curled the ball into the back of the net.

Jackson was the first to congratulate him. He was almost as happy as Callum!!

Callum was still grinning when the boys got back to their digs. He described every detail of his goal to Mrs Earls.

"I'm sure it'll be the first of many," said Mrs Earls.

"I hope so, ma'am," Callum replied. He quietly wondered what his dad would have thought.

Jackson felt a tinge of envy. Strikers always got the glory with their goals. No one paid much attention to holding midfielders.

But Jackson was soon to discover that drawing attention wasn't always a good thing...

CHAPTER FOUR

The final group game was against AC Milan and it was vital for both teams. Milan had beaten Sevilla 3–1, so they were level on points with Stanford. If Milan won, they would be the final. If Stanford won, they would be in the final. If it was a draw, a penalty shootout would decide the winner.

AC Milan was one of the most glamorous teams in the world with an amazing history. They had some huge stars. For Jackson, it was going to be a dream come true to play on the same pitch as them, and especially to be near one player in particular: Milan's good luck charm and captain, Abedi Afful.

Afful had been named African Player of the Year three times and had twice been runner-up for the Ballon d'Or. He was one of Jackson's idols.

For days, Jackson had dreamed of swapping shirts with Abedi at the end of the match.

When the two sides came out onto the pitch for their pre-match warm ups, Jackson kept glancing across to watch Abedi in action. Everything he did was so easy and graceful. He looked as if he'd been born with a ball at his foot.

Ron Grant talked about Afful in his team talk. He called him AC Milan's 'fulcrum', explaining that it meant Afful was the most important part of the team. All the play came through him and it was Jackson's job to stop him.

Stop Abedi Afful! How could he do that? Surely it was a task for an experienced player, like Mani Gronier? But Grant insisted that it was Jackson's job.

Grant looked Jackson straight in the eye and said "You can do this. AC Milan are an ageing team and Afful isn't getting any younger. It's time to make room for some new talent. He's had his time. Now this is yours."

Jackson usually had a few nerves before a game, but nothing like today. Today, he felt sick. He picked up his phone and went to sit in the toilet for a few minutes before the team went out for the kick-off.

The manager had a rule that no messages were to be sent or read in the changing room, but some of the players used their phones to listen to music through headphones. Jackson put his in his ears and selected his dad's favourite song — *Analengo* by Papa Wemba. His dad had played it all the time when Jackson and Marissa were growing up. Jackson loved its happy energy. It was just what he needed.

Glancing at the screen, Jackson saw he had a message. Without thinking, he opened it. It was from his mum. Jackson's heartbeat raced as he read it:

We've had a break-in. The police are here. Marissa is —

The message cut off mid-sentence.

Marissa is what? Jackson wondered, panicking.

Had she been hurt? Had someone taken her? It had to be Blake and his gang who were responsible for the break-in.

I should never have threatened a gang leader, thought Jackson

There was a knock on the cubicle door.

"Jackson, time to go!" It was Jadon Brooks, Stanford's captain.

"Coming," Jackson replied.

His voice shook with worry and fear. How was he going to get through this match with that alarming text message in his head?

CHAPTER FIVE

The first half was a nightmare for Stanford and for Jackson in particular. He couldn't settle at all. Abedi Afful gave him the run around. Jackson tried to get close to him, but Abedi was too clever. He moved all over the pitch: right, left, centre. One minute, he picked up the ball from his back four, the next, he sprinted into the Stanford half to link up another attack. He was like a ghost — and he was haunting Jackson.

AC Milan were on top from the start. They took the lead in the tenth minute, unfortunately because of Jackson.

For once, he didn't need to mark Abedi, because Milan had a corner and the African playmaker took it. It was an inswinger from the left.

Jackson stood by the near post but during the break in play his mum's worrying text flashed into his head. He lost focus.

Jackson didn't react quickly enough when the Milan striker darted across in front of him and headed the ball towards the goal. Jackson tried to clear the ball, but instead he diverted it past the helpless keeper and into the net.

Jackson had scored an own goal and Milan were one up in a game that Stanford desperately needed to win.

Things soon went from bad to worse.

Midway through the first half, with Milan dominating the play, Jackson made a second fatal error. With a smart turn, Afful slipped away from his young marker and headed towards the goal. Gronier stepped across to block him, but Afful was too quick and glided past him and into the Stanford penalty box.

Jackson raced back to try to catch his idol.

As Afful lifted his foot to shoot, Jackson slid in to take the ball. But he mistimed his tackle and brought Afful to the ground. The referee blew his whistle and pointed to the spot.

It was a clear penalty. No one protested.

Jackson was shown a yellow card.

Moments later, Abedi Afful slotted the ball into the left-hand corner of the net, sending the keeper the wrong way, and Milan were two goals up.

When the referee whistled for half-time, there were some boos from the home fans and Jackson was sure they were aimed at him. He trudged off the pitch with his head down. He felt terrible. He'd let his team down. He'd let his family down. It was the worst moment of his life.

As Jackson reached the tunnel, he heard someone call his name, and looked up to see his sister, Marissa. Marissa! She waved both her fists in the air, as if urging him on.

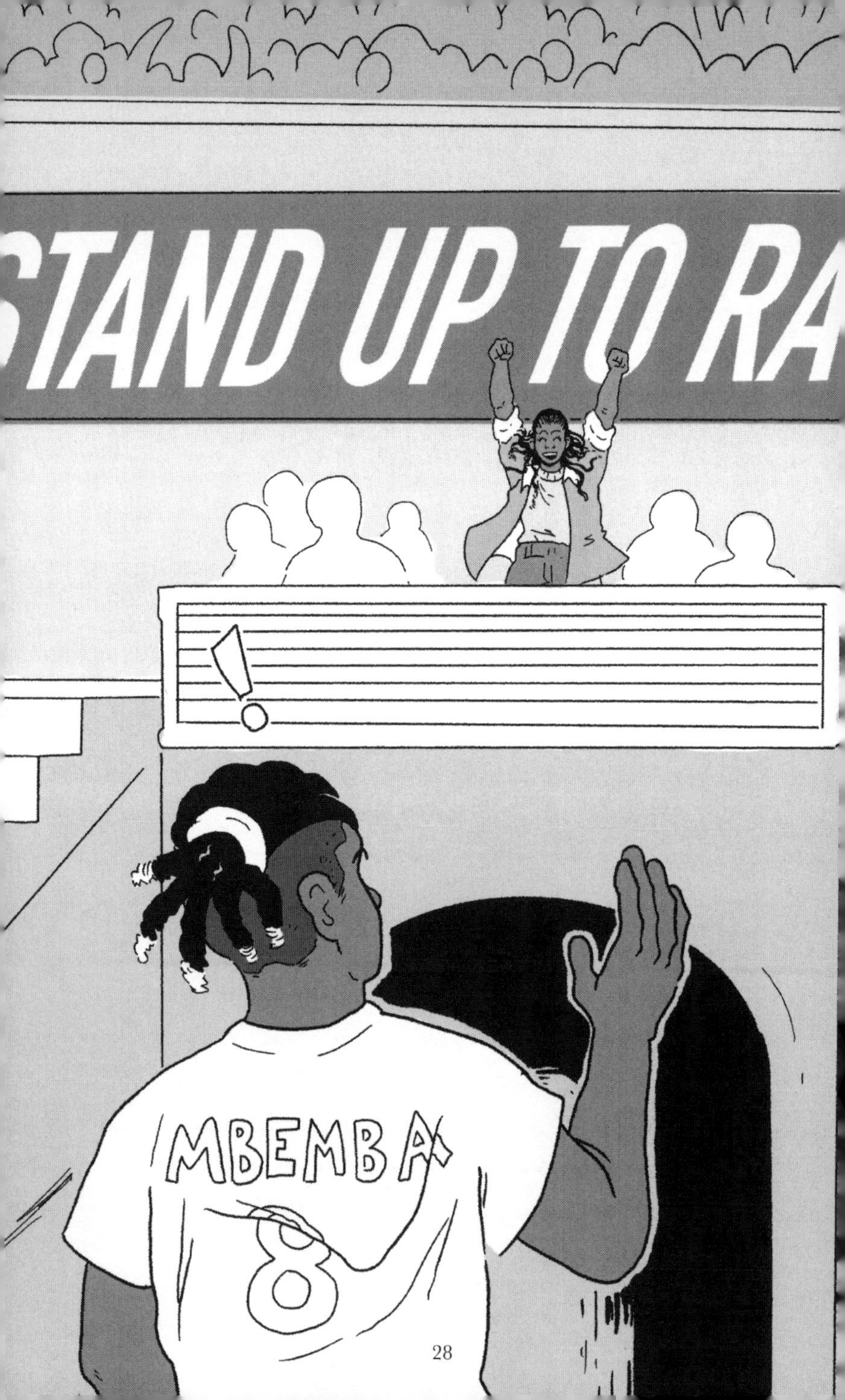
STAND UP TO RA
!
MBEMBA
8

Jackson felt such a wave of relief. His sister was okay. The missing bit of his mum's message must have said that Marissa was on the way to the match.

He didn't have to worry about her anymore!

Jackson's relief didn't last long though. It was soon replaced by misery as he thought about his awful first half. If only he hadn't looked at his mum's message before the game. If only the whole message had come through. If only he hadn't made those mistakes. If only...

But it was too late now. He'd messed up and he would have to pay the penalty. The manager would probably give him the boot and he'd have to watch Stanford struggle from the bench.

Ron Grant's half-time team talks were often angry but this time he was furious. He shouted and he swore. He kicked a shinpad across the changing room, narrowly missing club legend, Jorge Alvarez.

"DO BETTER," Grant fumed. "Do you even want to make the final? I need AT LEAST fifty percent more effort from everyone."

Grant announced that he wasn't changing any players yet.

"The team on the pitch caused this mess. Now go and fix it," he ordered.

Jackson was surprised the manager hadn't shouted at him for his mistakes, but as the players were preparing to take to the pitch for the second half, Grant pulled him aside.

"You were shocking in that first half, son. I should take you off. But I'm going to give you a second chance, because I believe in you," said Grant.

He gave Jackson a searching stare, continuing, "I just need you to show me that you believe in yourself."

He clapped his hand down on Jackson's shoulder. "Now, get out there and play."

CHAPTER SIX

Jackson couldn't believe his luck. He was still on the field. It was time for him to up his game.

At the manager's suggestion, Mani Gronier pushed forwards a little so that he and Jackson could work more as a pair to try to hold back Afful. It seemed to work too. With Gronier covering him, Jackson felt free to engage Afful. Early in the second half, he won the ball twice from his idol.

The next time the ball came towards him, Afful played it back rather than looking to break forwards. Milan started to look less dangerous. They sank deeper, deciding to hold on to what they had, which allowed Stanford more time on the ball.

Gronier's passes began hitting their mark, bringing Angelo into the game more.

It was from Angelo's pinpoint cross that Callum scored with a header, bringing Stanford back into the game.

Jackson was full of adrenalin now. He won headers, made tackle after tackle, and intercepted passes. He could sense that Afful was tiring which gave him the opportunity to surge forwards.

He set up Keller for a one-on-one with the Milan keeper, but his shot went wide.

Then the keeper saved a brilliant shot from Callum.

Milan started to look nervous. Their defender came in hard and mistimed a tackle, taking down Gronier who hit the ground with a thud. The ref blew his whistle and awarded a free kick to Stanford.

Gronier bent the free kick around the Milan wall but it hit the bar!

Time was running out.

Jorge Alvarez came on to join Callum and Reegan Keller up front, but they couldn't break down the Milan defence.

An official held up his board: two minutes of added time.

Stanford had a corner. Everyone, even the Stanford keeper, was in the Milan box.

The corner came in, but was headed away.

The ball dropped to Afful on the edge of the box and he was off. He didn't look tired now as he sprinted upfield.

Afful raced into the Stanford half, with an empty pitch and an empty goal in front of him. He was going to score!

Using all his energy, Jackson was after him.

As Afful approached the Stanford box, Jackson made his move. He had to time his tackle just right and he did, sliding across to take the ball away from his opponent. Then he was on his feet again and running towards the Milan goal.

Jackson passed to Gronier, who swung the ball hopefully into the Milan penalty area.

Jackson watched with his hands on his hips, gasping for breath.

The ball bounced off a defender's shin and fell into the path of Stanford's record goal scorer, Jorge Alvarez.

There was no way the Spaniard was going to miss. From two yards out, he toe-poked the ball home.

The stadium erupted. Stanford had drawn level with the last kick of the match!

The game was going to penalties.

Later, Ron Grant would say it was destiny that it was Jackson who took the fifth and final Stanford penalty with the scores level at 3–3.

The newspapers would say he had ice in his blood and nerves of steel.

But it didn't feel that way to Jackson when he stepped up and placed the ball on the spot.

Or when the ref blew his whistle.

Or when he trotted forwards, trying not to look at the goalie.

Or when he struck the ball towards the corner of the goal.

Only when the ball hit the back of the net did he feel an instant of calm.

Then came the roar of the crowd and the shouts of his teammates as they ran to hug him.

Jackson soaked up the moment.

Stanford were into the final of the Cathay Cup!

Further activities

1 Mrs Earls has many rules for the players staying at her house. Write a persuasive letter to Mrs Earls asking her to change one of her rules and the reasons why.

2 The Stanford vs. Milan match is filled with action. Create a comic-style storyboard to show the key events of the match.

Enjoyed this book?

Follow the Making the Team journey
across all six brilliant stories!

PAYING
THE PENALTY

Written by Alan Durant
Illustrated by Will Huck

Thanks to Inclusive Minds (the CIC supporting and championing inclusion and diversity in children's books) for introducing us to Kay and Gabriella through their network of Inclusion Ambassadors.

Special thanks also to Harrison, Parker and Reegan.

Titles in the Making the Team Series:
The Challenge
The Battle
Up and Running
Paying the Penalty
Taking a Stand
The Final

Badger Publishing Limited
Oldmedow Road,
Hardwick Industrial Estate,
King's Lynn PE30 4JJ

Telephone: **01553 816 082**
www.badgerlearning.co.uk

2 4 6 8 10 9 7 5 3 1

Paying the Penalty
ISBN 978-1-78837-658-7

Commissioning Editor: Sarah Rudd
Editor: Claire Morgan
Designer: Bigtop Design
Cover: alphaspirit.it/Shutterstock